There Are No Buffalo in Buffalo

A book of children's poems about places in New York State

by Sally Valentine

illustrated by Suzanne Valentine

Pyramid Publishing, Inc.
Utica, New York

ISBN-10 1-886166-35-8
ISBN-13 978-1-886166-35-6

Pyramid Publishing Inc.
PO Box 8339
Utica, New York 13505
www.pyramidpublishingservices.com

Ann - enjoy the collages - I learned so much creating them! ♡ Sue Valentine

I hope you enjoy this trip to the past & present.
Sally Valentine

In memory of my grandparents, Rudy and Emma Bandemer Valentine, and their families, who left Germany over 100 years ago looking for a better life. They came into America through Ellis Island and settled in western New York. Thanks to them I have lived my whole life in this beautiful state.

Ecclesiastes 3:11 He has made everything beautiful in its time.

BUFFALO

New York Blues

There are no buffalo in Buffalo,
Rye is not built of dark bread.
They don't grow almonds in Almond,
the bass in Fishkill are not dead.

So, is there silver in Sterling?
Can Sugar Loaf really be sweet?
Are there no long pants in Shortsville?
Is Redfield the color of beets?

Do they speak only German in Germantown?
Is there really a monarch in Queens?
I guess when it comes to the state of New York,
nothing is just as it seems.

Ausable Chasm

When lucky Lee's leg had a spasm,
he fell into Ausable Chasm.
        Hitting Elephant's Head,
        people thought he was dead.
But, broken bones Lee didn't have'em.

Historical Highlight: Ausable Chasm is a gorge carved in sandstone bedrock by the Ausable River as it flows from Mt. Marcy into Lake Champlain.

Adirondack Folk

Adirondacks don't use bricks.
They like their houses built from sticks.
Their beds, their chairs, their babies' shoes,
they're all made out of twigs and glue.

Wearing splinters on their feet
they ski along on wooden streets.
Antlers hang from all their rafters,
everyone's a handicrafter.

Stick cupboards hold their toothpick plates.
Have you ever lived in such a state?
Birch and pine fill all their homes.
I wonder . . . could they have stick bones?

Historical Highlight: New York's Adirondack Park was created in 1892 to help preserve the state's water and timber resources. Encompassing six million acres, it is larger than Yellowstone, Everglades, Glacier, and Grand Canyon National Park all put together.

Albany

Albany

In Albany the people meet;
every region has its seat.
They gather here to make new laws,
to plead their case, to flap their jaws.

Blueblood son or new arriver,
businessman or big rig driver.
All are represented here,
the unemployed, the store cashier.

Building highways, funding schools,
regulating power and fuel,
enforcing codes, imposing taxes,
poor folk falling through the crackses.

All things serve the great agenda,
meetings, lobbies, referenda.
Debating issues word by word.
How will you make your voice be heard?

Historical Highlight: Founded by the Dutch in 1624 as Fort Orange, Albany has been the capital of New York State since 1797.

Buffalo Wings

Buffalo is the city of lights,
Pierce Arrow cars and Frank Lloyd Wright,
beef on weck and other fine things,
but Buffalo lives on chicken wings.

Buffalo celebrates Dyngus Day,
polkas, pussy willows, and parades.
Pierogis, golobki may think they're king,
but Buffalo flies on chicken wings.

Logenberry is common fare,
Millard Fillmore is buried there,
Olmsted parks turn green in spring,
but Buffalo is famous for chicken wings.

Historical Highlight: Buffalo is the second largest city in New York State. In 1964 at the Anchor Bar Restaurant, Teressa Bellissimo made the first ever Buffalo wings flavored with her secret sauce.

Brooklyn Bridge

spans the East River
and three centuries.
Built to last with strong steel cables
and Gothic towers, it still elevates the lives
of those who step, bike, or drive across its great suspense.
Pedestrians, carriages, horses and riders, livestock, trolleys, trains, cars, bikes, and
even 21 elephants (I swear it's true) have crossed from Manhattan to Brooklyn
or from Brooklyn
over to Manhattan
Just to ex perience
poetry in motion.

Historical Highlight: Taking thirteen years to construct, the Brooklyn Bridge was the world's first steel-wire suspension bridge. 150,300 people walked across it on opening day, May 24, 1883.

Beaverkill Beaverkill
Beaverkill beaverkill beaverkill
Beaverkill Beaverkill
beaverkill

Beaverkill

Those dam beavers are at it again!
Gnawing, chopping, felling,
alder, poplar, willow,
taking my home to fashion their own.

Those dam builders are at it again!
Patching, plugging, stopping
up my stream with their logging,
forcing me to dip my ladle elsewhere.

Those dam beavers are at it again!
Thwack! Smack! Thwack!
Announcing me as enemy at the gate.
How can we be good neighbors?

Historical Highlight: The beaver is the official mammal of New York State. It is the largest rodent in North America. The term "kil" is Dutch for creek or stream.

Chautauqua

Modern pretenders
toss words into sacred space.
God rains poetry.

Historical Highlight: Chautauqua is synonymous with the arts. For nine weeks in summer, the Chautauqua Institution offers courses and provides forums for art, music, dance, theater, and writing.

The Cardiff Giant

The Cardiff Giant was a hoax,
a pretend man, a fossil joke.
But facts did not stop some people
from paying up to get a peep full.

Atheist Hull meant to poke fun
of Bible believers, but he was outdone
by P.T. Barnum who proceeded to take
and make himself a fake of a fake.

So two fake men both carved from stone
attracted crowds, became well known.
Now we may as well just admit it:
"There's a sucker born every minute."

Historical Highlight: On October 16, 1869, well diggers dug up a 2,990 pound, 10-foot-tall petrified man in Cardiff, NY. It was planted there the previous year by the owner's cousin who wanted to make fun of people who believed that giants once inhabited earth. The Cardiff Giant is now on display at the Farmer's Museum in Cooperstown, NY.

central park

Central Park

Come!
Worship with me in Central Park where
God and Mr. Olmsted created an elm cathedral,
Cleopatra's needle points to heaven, and
200 bird families make a pilgrimage
each year just to harmonize with the choir.

The Word is spoken in the silence of Poet's Walk,
an angel continually blesses the healing water of Bethesda.
The flock can lie down in the green pastures of Sheep Meadow
or rest beside the still waters of Harlem Meer.

Balto testifies to daily sacrifice and
the carousel rings with eternity.
Come!
Climb on the rocks of ages or
wander through Strawberry Fields.
Just
Imagine.

Historical Highlight: Central Park encompasses 843 acres and 51 city blocks in Manhattan. It contains 21 playgrounds, 29 sculptures, 1,700 elm trees, and 9,000 park benches.

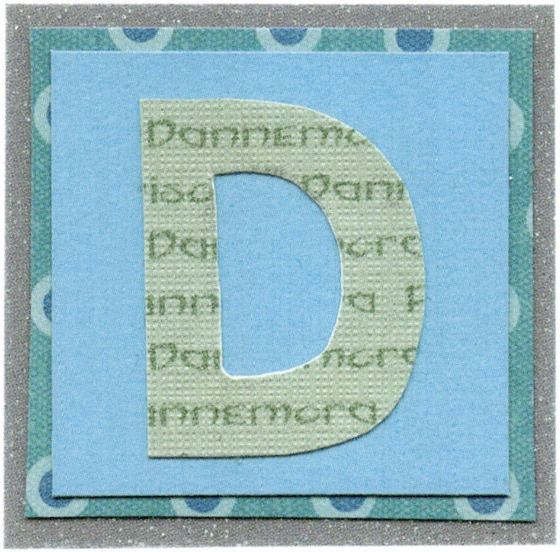

Deposit

Years ago, deposits of logs
waited on river banks for spring
and a ride down the Delaware.

Nowdays, deposits of water
wait for word from city slickers.
"We're thirsty. Send water here."

Mother Earth provides for her children.

Historical Highlight: Once known for logging, the town of Deposit is now known for its reservoir that supplies drinking water to New York City.

Fort Drum

Fort Drum soldiers build bridges in Iraq.
Starting at the base of selfless service,
they pile up bricks of duty and respect,
stack them on loyalty and honor,
hold them together with courage and integrity,
creating paths where once were gaps,
engineering a new future for two peoples.
Fort Drum soldiers build bridges in Iraq.

Historical Highlight: Fort Drum is a U.S. Army base outside of Watertown, NY. Its 107,000 acres are home to the 10th Mountain Division. Eighty thousand troops are trained there each year.

Dannemora Prison

Dannemora Prison Blues

Stuck here in this cell. Hell!
When I'll get out – no tell.
May just have to stay a spell
in this dumbbell hotel.

Busted on a bum rap,
caught up in a police trap.
All I wanted was a hubcap.
Now I'm in the law's lap.

Though I'm cured of TB,
hand me up that passkey.
I ain't no bad like Bucky.
Won't somebody free me?

Historical Highlight: Clinton Correctional Facility in Dannemora, NY, is a maximum security prison for men. Inmates with tuberculosis have been cured there by the clear mountain air.

Etna

In Etna there's trouble a brewing.
The people are frothing and spewing.
    Their post office gone,
    they'll have to log on
to send word about why they're stewing.

Historical Highlight: Etna, in Tompkins County, was named for the volcano in Sicily. In 2011, the U.S. Postal Service was planning to close the post office in Etna. People's protests stalled the move.

Erie Canal

Welcome to my waters.
I am your Erie Canal.
Don't call me Clinton's Dirty Ditch!
I am a living legend.
I am an engineering marvel,
dug by men who
mowed through miles of forest,
stood chest deep in mosquitoed swamp
making elevators for water.

Helped by horses and handmade tools,
paid in cheap wages and cheap whiskey,
they laid a new road in America,
creating kinship in Albany and Buffalo,
marrying Lake Erie to Atlantic Ocean.

I was born of their labor, and then
gave birth myself,
flour mills, lumber mills, knitting mills,
breweries, carpet factories, salt mines.

Today I let down my locks to you.
Take a trip through my territory,
cast a line in my direction,
park your pack boat and sit under my spell.
Lade for yourself cotton and coal, wares
and wheat.
Learn from me.
I have the wisdom that old age brings.
I am a living legend.
I am your Erie Canal.

Historical Highlight: The Erie Canal was designed and built without the help of a single trained engineer. Workers made their own tools and battled malaria and rattlesnakes to carve a water route between the Hudson River in Albany and Lake Erie in Buffalo. The canal opened in 1825, bringing people, goods, and prosperity to New York State.

ellis island ellis island ellis island ellis island ellis island ellis island

Ellis Island

Coming to America

My grandpa's grandpa
    came through Ellis Island.
How about yours?
Led by wonder and the White Star
he steamed across the ocean,
spilled out with teams of others
seeking orchards of opportunity
on America's ripe shores.

Wearing his best (only) suit with
an inspection sticker boutonnière,
he passed the six second physical
after being button-hooked
    for tell-tale eyes.
He aced the twenty-nine question quiz
answering "yes" to job? and can read?
"no" to polygamist? anarchist?
    and debtor?

He dragged bags and babies
    up the Great Hall,
stood his place in the line
of new Americans adding
his native German to the babble.

He walked proudly out of
    the Immigration Station
with membership card and
new home tailored to fit his family.

My grandpa's grandpa
    came through Ellis Island.
How about yours?

Historical Highlight: Over twelve million immigrants entered the United States through Ellis Island between 1892 and 1954. Over 40% of Americans can trace a relative through Ellis Island.

Finger Lakes

Some say the Finger Lakes
were created by glaciers.
North running streams and
south stretching ice floes
married for a few thousand years
giving birth to long, skinny children
with deep roots in Western New York.

But the Iroquois say
the lakes are the imprint
of the Great Spirit who lovingly
reached out from heaven
to caress the land He created.

Who says God only has ten fingers?

Historical Highlight: Western New York has eleven long, slender lakes that look like fingers when viewed from above. They are, from west to east, Conesus, Hemlock, Canadice, Honeoye, Canandaigua, Keuka, Seneca, Cayuga, Owasco, Skaneateles, and Otisco.

Fort Ticonderoga

Lock the gate, soldier.
Lock up the fort well.
Lock the gate, soldier.
Heed this tale I tell

'bout Ben and Ethan
and those green hilled boys
who captured a fort
like a small Tinkertoy.

They snuck 'cross Champlain
in the dark of the night,
walked right through the gate
without even a fight.

While the Brits were asleep
Ticonderoga fell.
So stay awake, soldiers.
Lock up the fort well.

Historical Highlight: On May 10, 1775, Ethan Allen and Benedict Arnold led the Green Mountain Boys in the first offensive victory for the Colonists in the Revolutionary War. They walked through the unlocked gate and took Fort Ticonderoga without firing a single shot.

fire island lighthouse

Fire Island Lighthouse

Faithful Servant,
you've served your country well.
Countless were the hours
you spent towering over
    our port and our past,
spine of iron,
muscles of rock,
guardian of the gateway,
silent sentinel.
Speaking to our fathers in waves of light,
you never left your post
for warmer climes or calmer coasts.

Now some call you obsolete,
deplete you of your former fame,
reduce you to a useless has-been,
dismiss your very right to exist.

But I say, "Stand tall, Old Soldier."
Your eyes still welcome
    New Yorkers home.
In your light, those with vision
see the reservoirs of our past
refracted into our future.
"Stand tall, Old Soldier."
We salute you.

Historical Highlight: The first lighthouse on Fire Island was completed in 1826.
The current lighthouse is visible for more than twenty miles.

Gloversville

Hands that once tanned hide,
cut skins, stitched leather,
now stretch out for new
industry custom
fit for skilled fingers.

Historical Highlight: From 1890–1950, ninety percent of gloves sold in America were made in Gloversville.

Racing The Glen

Gun it at the green flag,
jump ahead of the crush,
muffle out road noise,
listen to the hum of your own engine.
Lean right into The Ninety.
Then head for The Esses,
watching out for sideswipers and hubcap lockers.
You can kiss the curb,
but stay away from the wall.
Make up time on the Back Straight,
but don't be a meatball,
use caution going into the Busstop.
Circle that Inner Loop,
then slide down The Chute and
watch those trains stand still.
Make a pit stop if you must,
but then shift back to the asphalt.
Brake on The Toe,
but don't get The Boot.
You're geared up for the home stretch,
the checkered flag is waving at you.
No more Andretti and Petty.
YOU own The Glen now.

Historical Highlight: The Watkins Glen International is New York State's premier auto racetrack and one of only a few road tracks in the country. It celebrated its 60th anniversary in 2008.

Rome New York
ROME
ALL ROADS LEAD TO...

Greece and Rome

Did you ever want to travel to Greece
or see the sights of Rome?
Thanks to New York's classical state,
visit Europe without leaving home.

Hop on the Thruway at Ilion,
head west to Verona and Rome.
Manlius, Marcellus, Camillus,
use Fabius for your stepping stone.

Over to Ithaca, Ovid.
Pompey and Cato and more.
If you're looking for classical places,
New York is the state to explore.

Historical Highlight: After the Revolutionary War, New York State set aside land known as the Military Tract in the middle of the state to be given to veterans as payment for their service. Robert Harpur, a deputy secretary of state and the land commissioners divided up the land and gave each parcel a classical name.

Howe Caverns Haiku

Stalactites bite down,
Limestone fangs in Nature's jaw,
Stalagmites strike up.

Historical Highlight: Howe Caverns is located in Schoharie County just northeast of Cobleskill. Lester Howe uncovered the entrance to the caverns on May 5, 1842, while tending his cows. The cows were attracted by the cool air rising from the caverns where the underground temperature is 52°.

Herkimer Diamonds

New York is a gem
of a state where Herkimer
diamonds rival the real thing. Hiding for
500 million years in dull dolomite, growing stronger
than steel, these stepstones are ready now
to show all 18 faces to the world.
Go pick out a beauty.

Historical Highlight: Herkimer "diamonds" are really quartz crystals that are embedded in dolomite rock in the area around Herkimer, NY.

APOLLO
APOLLO

Harlem

It's amateur night at the Apollo.
A-trainers bump-a-dance down
the Boulevard of Dreams to 125th Street
and a chance at fame.
Aspiring artists hiphop
their way on stage,
touching the Tree of Hope just for luck.
Ethel and Ella, Nat King Cole and the Duke
all found their way here,
feasting at Fabian's or Frank's,
but thirsting for success.
The Harlem Renaissance is not over.
Tap the Tree of Hope and strut your stuff.
Somebody's a winner on Wednesday night.

Historical Highlight: The Apollo Theater in Harlem has been holding Amateur night since 1934.

Iroquois Indian Museum

Corn, Squash, Beans,
Yellow, Orange, Green,
    Sisters entwined,
    On ground or on vine,
Corn, Squash, Beans.

Historical Highlight: The Iroquois were the first inhabitants of New York State. They grew corn, squash, and beans, calling them the three sisters.

Intrepid

The USS Intrepid was fearless,
fighting major World War II battles,
surviving kamikaze attacks,
coming back wounded to win the Pacific War.

Resurrected from retirement,
fighting in Korea and Viet Nam,
it's recovered Navy men
astronauts, and
New Yorkers traumatized by terrorists.

New Yorkers: just call us intrepid.

Historical Highlight: The aircraft carrier, USS Intrepid, launched in 1943 during World War II, has been reconditioned and was re-opened as a museum in the New York City harbor on Nov. 11, 2008.

Ithaca
Ithaca Ithaca Ithaca Ithaca
Ithaca Ithaca
Ithaca

Ithaca

Ithaca is an ice cream sundae
sitting high above the bowl of Cayuga Lake.
Creeks of sweet water flow like hot fudge or strawberry sauce,
cutting colorful gorges into the creamy vanilla landscape.
Art and music cover it all,
enriching life like real whipped cream.
(not the cheap chemical imitation)
Cornell is simply the cherry on top.
Bring a spoon and dig in!

Historical Highlight: Ithaca claims to be the home of the first ice cream sundae, served to the Rev. John M. Scott in the Platt and Colt Pharmacy on a Sunday in 1892.

Jamaica

Jamaica lies at a crossroads
where people are coming and going.
Dirt paths bore produce by cartloads.
Jamaica lies at a crossroads.
Now rails commute workers by trainloads.
Traffic shows no signs of slowing.
Jamaica lies at a crossroads
where people are coming and going.

Historical Highlight: Jamaica is a neighborhood of 200,000 people in Queens, NY. Lying along an ancient trail, it continues to be a transportation hub, with a central station of the Long Island Railroad and an airtrain to JFK airport.

Jamestown Fame

Jamestown's proud of all its clan
from every walk of life,
starting with James Pendergast
and first mayor Oscar Price.

Jamestown applauds for Merchants,
proudly boasts those Maniacs.
It likes all things theatrical,
will not forget amnesiacs.

Jamestown brags on birder Peterson
for him they're sprucey goosey.
Jamestown's proud of all its kin,
But, oh how they love Lucy.

Historical Highlight: Comedienne Lucille Ball was born in Jamestown, NY, on August 6, 1911. Jamestown is home to the Lucille Ball-Desi Arnaz Center and holds a Lucy festival every year.

Jones Beach Jones Beach Jones Beach Jones Beach
Jones Beach Jones Beach Jones Beach Jones Beach
Jones Beach Jones Beach Jones Beach Jones Beach
Jones Beach Jones Beach Jones Beach Jones Beach
Jones Beach Jones Beach Jones Beach Jones Beach

Jones Beach
A Tale of Two Seasons

Jones Beach sparkles in summer,
sun reflecting diamonds in the sand.
Worshippers stretch for seven miles,
    swimming, whimming,
    splashing, dashing
    into the waves.
Every day is Independence Day.

In January the beach is lonely,
concert stage stands empty,
beach blankets blown away,
fireworks fizzled out.
But if you chance to walk the strand,
water will still wash over your feet,
sand will still seep between your toes,
and the tide will still
    roll in, roll out,
    roll in, roll out,
loyal even in the off season.

Historical Highlight: Jones Beach State Park is located on the southern shore of Long Island. With six and a half miles of beach and two miles of boardwalk, it attracts eight million visitors a year.

Knowlesville

Nobody knows about Knowlesville.
It's a secret that's very well kept.
What nobody knows about Knowlesville
is that nobody knows were it's et.

Historical Highlight: Knowlesville (population 275) is in Orleans County.

Kinderhook

Martin Van Buren

Our eighth American president.
Lived a fine life – that's evident.
Definitely drawn from Dutch descent.

Kindled Democratic Party ascent.
Innkeeper's son and country gent.
New York's political instrument.
Defended each state's right to dissent.
Elegantly dressed wherever he went.
Restricting slave states was his intent.
Hannah, his wife, came heaven sent.
Opposed adding Texas to our complement.
Organized voters to give their consent.
Kinderhook's most famous resident.

Historical Highlight: New York State has been home to four U. S. Presidents: Martin Van Buren, Millard Fillmore, Theodore Roosevelt, and Franklin Roosevelt. All except Fillmore also served as New York State Governor. Grover Cleveland also spent many years in NYS, serving both as mayor of Buffalo and governor before becoming president.

Kingston
Shad Festival

Kingston Shad

The river was full of anadromous
fish when Hendrick Hudson strayed,
got lost on his way to Asia
and sailed upriver a ways.

For years and years the rivermen
cast their fishing nets with care.
In with forsythia, out with the lilacs,
hundreds of herring to spare.

Now fewer shad still come home to spawn,
and the Hudson cries tears of sadness.
Oh, what a tragical state of affairs!
Shad Festival has now become shadless.

Historical Highlight: Kingston was the first capital of New York State (1777–1789). It is home to the Hudson Maritime Museum, which hosts a shad festival every year in the spring when the shad (herring) come upriver to spawn. In recent years the number of shad has dwindled so that the Shad Festival has become shadless.

Leroy From LeRoy

Leroy from LeRoy was such an odd fellow.
He studied a lot and ate nothing but Jell-O.

His mother would yell and his father would bellow,
but Leroy from LeRoy would eat only Jell-O.

He memorized Hamlet, King Lear, and Othello
all the while slurping down gallons of Jell-O.

He played the piano, the flute, harp, and cello
practicing in between spoonfuls of Jell-O.

His body turned softer, his brain stretched and
swelled so,
but Leroy from LeRoy kept on eating Jell-O.

'Til one day he burst, that pathetic, odd fellow,
dissolved in a pool of lime green, orange, and yellow.

Historical Highlight: Jell-O was invented in 1897 in LeRoy, NY by Pearle B. Wait, a cough syrup manufacturer, and his wife, May Davis West.

Levittown

Mr.Levitt built some houses for families after the European war.
Stamped out one right after the other on a production line,
It was hard to tell one from its twin next door.

Concrete slab, wood frame, roof, door, window, stove, washer, fridge.
Concrete slab, wood frame, roof, door, window, stove, washer, fridge.
Concrete slab, wood frame, roof, door, window, stove, washer, fridge.

Thirty houses a day popped out of the factory and onto an
old Long Island potato farm, creating a neigh bor hood that
looked kind of like this. Presto! Chango! Suburbia was born.

Historical Highlight: Between 1947 and 1951, Abraham Levitt and his sons built 17,447 mass-produced houses on twelve hundred acres of potato farmland on Long Island. This development was the first mass-produced suburban community in the country.

LOON LAKE

Loon Lake

Listen to the lonely call of the loon.
Wha ha ha oo oo. Wha ha ha oo oo.
Calling his mate, "Come home here to roost."
Wha ha ha oo oo. Wha ha ha oo oo.
"Together we'll raise a family or two."
Wha ha ha oo oo. Wha ha ha oo oo.

Listen to the lonely call of the loon.
Whoo oo. Whoo oo. Whoo oo. Whoo oo.
Calling his friends to waddle the marshland.
Whoo oo. Whoo oo. Whoo oo. Whoo oo.
A fishing party is what they have planned.
Whoo oo. Whoo oo. Whoo oo. Whoo oo.

Listen to the lonely call of the loon.
Whahahahaha. Whahahahaha.
Warning the others that danger lurks by.
Whahahahaha. Whahahahaha.
Watch out! Watch out! Snapping turtle is nigh.
Whahahahaha. Whahahahaha.

Listen to the lonely call of the loon.
Wha ha ha. Wha ha ha. Wha ha ha ha.
Singing the song that rose from the glaciers.
Wha ha ha. Wha ha ha. Wha ha ha ha.
It echoes today in lakes clean and pure.
Wha ha ha. Wha ha ha. Wha ha ha ha.

Listen to the lonely call of the loon.
Is he speaking to me?
Is he speaking to you?
Wha ha ha he. Wha ha ha hoo.

Historical Highlight: The common loon inhabits the Adirondack lakes in summer. It has four different calls: a unique yodel, a hoot to call other loons, a wail to warn of danger, and a tremolo to show fear.

Driving Manhattan

Driving Manhattan is crazy.
Hang on tight;
don't go too slow.
Zigzag 'round jay walkers,
shake your fist at the gawkers,
and use all the swear words you know.

Driving Manhattan is crazy.
Start with a prayer;
Lord have mercy.
Then lay on your horn,
but just be forewarned,
you may have to park in New Jersey.

Historical Highlight: Parking spaces are hard to find in Manhattan. In 2007, NYC collected $530 million in parking fees.

Montezuma Zuma

The days were getting shorter as they're wont to do in fall,
when Zuma became restless; she'd heard Mother Nature call.
She got her things together, as such there was to get,
for osprey must pack lightly when embarking on a trip.

She taxied the wet runway and soon was in the air,
she circled once and headed south, the route that she'd prepared.
Her GPS was working as the miles stripped away.
She reached the Carolinas' coast in just a couple days.
And then flew on to Florida, with a flutter and a whish.
She only stopped just here and there, wherever she could fish.
Caracas followed Cuba; she ticked them off her list.
Guyana led on to Brazil, she'd finally found her bliss.

Zuma stayed the whole long winter, unending Mardi Gras,
but then that traveler's fever started sticking in her craw.
She thought of Montezuma and her home within the fen,
she got herself together, and went back there once again.
As the journey took her northward, Zuma had some time to ponder.
I guess my fate will always be to migrate and to wander.

Historical Highlight: Established in 1938 with 7,000 acres of marshland, the Montezuma National Wildlife Refuge at the north end of Cayuga Lake is a refuge and breeding ground for migratory waterfowl. Officials there tracked an osprey they named Zuma on her migratory path from NY to South America.

Mt Marcy

Mt. Marcy

Even amateurs can climb Mt. Marcy;
just start moving and you'll get your groove.
Jump over streams,
watch out for sharp rocks,
don't worry when you can't see
the top through the wall of trees.
Keep going and you'll break through
to the summit.

Then shout out your name.

Hear it echo off Algonquin and Colden.
Watch it fall into Lake Tear of the Woods.
Hold your breath as it catches
the Hudson current, and bow
your head as it passes the
Statue of Liberty, finally
leaping out into the great Atlantic,
announcing to the world
that you have arrived.

*Historical Highlight: New York State has 46 peaks over 4,000 feet tall.
Mt. Marcy, at 5,344 feet, is the highest point in the state.*

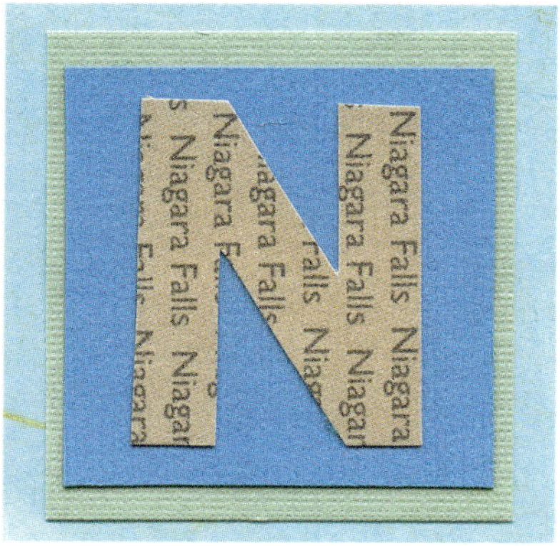

New York Stock Exchange

When trading stocks you'd better prepare
to declare yourself a bull or a bear.
Thinking that stocks will continue to rise,
being a bull, you'll continue to buy.
But, thinking investors better beware,
you won't dare to buy cause the market's a bear.

Historical Highlight: The New York Stock Exchange traces its roots to a 1792 agreement made by twenty-four stockbrokers underneath a buttonwood tree on Wall Street in New York City.

N-titled

Some N towns are named for great people:
Newtonville, Newcomb and Nichols.
Others recall foreign places:
New Bremen, New Brighton, and Naples.

Towns like Nunda, Niobe, and Nyack
have names that just make you think.
Some names give geographic location:
Natural Bridge, North Creek, Neversink.

But my favorite of all the N names
is a place that you prob'ly don't know
was named because Worden was taken,
so backwards it changed to Nedrow.

Historical Highlight: New York State has forty-one places that either begin with the word New or have New as a prefix.

Niagara Falls

Visit to Niagara Falls

Buy a T-shirt.
Take lots of pictures.
Step across the Rainbow to
dip a foot into Canada.

But then...
stop and listen
        to the river's voice,
stand and look
        into the gorge's eyes,
stretch and lift
        your tongue to taste the water's kiss.

Ride on the back of the rapids if you're able, and
sit for just a moment in the lap of the Almighty.

Historical Highlight: Comprised of the American Falls and Bridal Veil Falls on the American side of the Niagara River and by Horseshoe Falls on the Canadian side, the falls are renowned for providing both beauty and hydroelectric power.

Ontario County Courthouse Rock

Treaty rock remembers pledges of peace, friendship, and free passage brokered by Pickering, Corn Planter, Quakers.

Writing in stone and two-row wampum belt, they swapped peace, cash, and calico. Men may forget, but rock remembers.

Historical Highlight: On November 11, 1794, a peace treaty was signed between the Iroquois nation and the U.S. government. As part of this agreement, the U.S. government still gives the Haudenosaunee $4,500 and bolts of cloth every year. A rock on the courthouse lawn in Canandaigua, NY commemorates the spot where the treaty was signed.

Onondaga Nation

Lacrosse

L	A	C	R	O	S	S	E	S	T	I	L	**L**
H	**A**	S	S	A	C	R	E	D	P	L	**A**	Y.
H	I	**C**	K	O	R	Y	S	T	I	**C**	K	S
P	A	I	**R**	P	L	A	Y	E	**R**	S	T	O
T	H	E	H	**O**	L	Y	M	**O**	T	H	E	R
E	A	R	T	H.	**S**	O	**S**	T	R	O	N	G
A	R	E	T	H	E	**S**	P	I	R	I	T	S
T	H	E	Y	G	**E**	N	**E**	R	A	T	E	A
W	E	L	L	**S**	P	O	T.	**S**	H	O	U	T
O	U	T	**T**	O	C	R	E	A	**T**	O	R'	S
P	R	**I**	M	A	L	H	E	A	L	**I**	N	G.
S	**C**	O	R	E	A	N	D	W	A	T	**C**	H
K	I	N	S	M	E	N'	S	S	P	A	R	**K**.

Historical Highlight: The Onondaga Nation is a separate entity totally surrounded by the state of New York. Members of the Haudenosaunee, or Iroquois, the Onondaga Nation is ruled by a Council of Chiefs. Lacrosse, which is sacred to the Haudenosaunee, is the oldest team sport in North America.

Lake Ontario

Lake Ontario

I am the little brother,
afterthought,
tag-a-long,
wearing hand-me-downs from Huron,
mistreated by Michigan,
agitated by Erie,
totally upstaged by my biggest brother
who thinks he's so Superior.

But I have a secret –
Mother Nature loves me best.

Historical Highlight: Lake Ontario is the smallest of the five Great Lakes of North America. Both Lake Ontario and Lake Erie lie partially within New York's border. The Great Lakes contain approximately 20% of the world's fresh surface water.

Painted Post

Bury me down by the rivers,
where Cohocton and Tioga meet.
Paint up a post for remembrance.
Then cover me up with a sheet.

Historical Highlight: Painted Post is situated where the Cohocton River and Tioga River meet to form the Chemung River. Early settlers came upon a red pole that had twenty-eight figures of men carved into it. No one knows how or why it came to be there.

A Paradox in Paradox

On a parasol day in Paradox,
things move along just the way they ought.
Water flows downstream from lake to river,
river receiver, and lake the giver.

But in years when Paradox puddles in rain,
water will flow in an opposite vein.
The lake that was giving is now the one getting,
the inletting river is now found outletting.

Historical Highlight: Paradox in Essex County was so named because of the unusual geographic phenomenon described in the poem.

lake placid
ski trails
ice skating

Lake Placid

Lake Placid is a town of winners,
where iron men and women compete
against the elements and each other
for the gold, the silver and the bronze,
setting world records
for speed and style and endurance.

Every day is a miracle on ice,
where even common folk are transported
by dogsled, bobsled, skate, and ski.
Mirror Lake quietly reflects the joy
of just frolicking in Jack Frost's
white-faced playground.

Historical Highlight: Lake Placid, NY has hosted the Winter Olympics twice, in 1932 and again in 1980.

Quaker Street

Friends meet here
seeking God's Spirit,
then go forth
as equals,
finding God in each person,
simply living peace.

Historical Highlight: Quaker Street is a hamlet in Schenectady County where sixty-one Quaker homes and businesses from the 19th century have been preserved.

Queens

One Immigrant's Story

Quentin found a quarter
on a quiet quay in Queens.
He stuffed it in his pocket
and said, "I'm a man of means."

The other kids all laughed at him.
"Dumb Quentin thinks he's rich."
When every other Queens' kid knows
two bits can't buy a stitch.

But Quentin didn't listen,
he didn't seem concerned.
He kept collecting quarters,
some he found, but most he earned.

And soon that little quarter
grew into a dollar bill.
One dollar grew to several
and kept on growing 'til...

Quentin had so much money that
he bought his folks a home,
two cars, a grand piano,
and a trip from Queens to Rome.

Quentin even bought a steamship
that he captains out to sea,
and just before he climbs on board,
he drops a quarter on the quay.

*Historical Highlight: The borough of Queens is the most diverse place in America.
In 2005, over 47% of its residents were immigrants. There are 138 languages spoken there.*

Quogue Quogue Quogue Quogue Quogue Quogue Quogue

Quogue

How many clams for a Quogue clam?
How many clams would you pay?
For a taste of the sea
It's a treat, yesiree!
The finest in all of the land.

Historical Highlight: Long Island owes much of its history and culture to hard clams, which are harvested from the muddy bottoms of the coastal waters. Hard clams come in three sizes: chowder (largest), cherrystone (mid-sized), and littleneck (smallest).

I'd Rather be Rich

How can I choose between Richburg,
Richfield, Richford, or Richville?
I guess any town that starts Richly,
will fit the bill and fill the till.

Historical Highlight: Richfield in Otsego County was named for the quality of the soil there.

Rochester

Rochester lives for lilac time
when Spring finally gives
    Winter the boot and
Highland Park develops
    from black and white
into frames of color.
She's been silently preparing for weeks
for her yearly Open House,
the biggest splash of the
    New York festival season.

Dressed not just in purple,
but also white, pink, and blue with
pansy accents and
    rhododendron accessories,
she's ready to dazzle.
Admirers come from miles around and
Suitors parade back and forth
simply to pay homage to her beauty,
hoping to be favored with a smile
she has reserved for them alone.

But heed this hard earned warning:
Just one whiff of her perfume
    can be intoxicating,
filling one's head with ideas of
    picnics and poems,
    castles and creampuffs,
    fables and ferries.
Draw close at your own risk.
It's a rare man who can
resist her charms.

Historical Highlight: Rochester is the third largest city in New York State.
Rochester's Highland Park boasts 111 acres of 500 different varieties of lilacs.
The Lilac Festival, held every May, draws thousands of visitors to the park.

Romulus friends

Romulus Friends

In Romulus the brown deer and white deer are friends.

They run together
tramping the same trails,
leaping over the same streams,
flag tails waving at the same scent of danger.
Captives of the cold war,
yet as free as God's grace,
they stand nose to nose
on the hills between the sacred lakes,
licking kisses.
At night they bed together peacefully
atop concrete igloos that hold cast off
weapons of another species.

In Romulus the white deer and brown deer are friends.

Historical Highlight: An unusual herd of over two hundred white deer inhabit the site of the former Seneca Army Depot in Romulus, New York. They share the land with brown (whitetail) deer and other wildlife.

Syracuse Orangemen

In Syracuse, the Orangemen rule
the town. They own the school.
Running the floor, making the score,
teaming up against Green,
dribbling circles around Blue,
jumping over Redheads,
sinking one, two, three point shots
every time into the basket.
Treading the hardwood
right in the face of Purple
rebounding past Gray to
slam-dunk Gold at the buzzer.
In Syracuse, the Orangemen got game.

Historical Highlight: Syracuse University is a private school founded in 1870. Its athletes are known as the Orangemen or Orangewomen or simply the Orange. The school mascot is Otto the Orange.

Saratoga Springs

Saratoga is a town of thoroughbreds,
young trotters racing round the track,
old gray mares bubbling up in mineral water,
Skidmore students studying the arts and themselves,
ballet dancers tiptoeing between the trees,
musicians jamming up sidewalk cafes,
artists and writers coloring in the shadow of Yaddo,
revolutionaries re-enacting bitter battles.
Saratoga is a town of thoroughbreds.

Historical Highlight: Saratoga Springs dates back to 1767 when Native Americans led a British soldier, Sir William Johnson, to High Rock Spring for healing of his war wounds. The area became known for its mineral water spas in the 1800s.

House Deed
Owner:
Mary Smith
Lake of Liberty
WOMEN
Vote Today!

Seneca Falls Daughters

In a quiet church in a quiet town
a century of men and women
shout out a new gospel of independence.
Elizabeth and Lucretia lead a new role call
declaring women equal (under God) to men.
Boldy they dare daughters and wives to
    stake out a claim to own property,
    step out of long skirts into bloomers,
    walk out of kitchens into voting booths.
Change links to change.
Cause begets cause.
    Give Women the Vote!
    Abolish Slavery!
    Forbid Alcohol!
Every stream of conscience
joins the river of reform,
stumbles over rocks of opposition,
eventually empties into the lake of liberty.
"Failure is impossible."

Historical Highlight: In 1848 the first Women's Rights Convention was held in Seneca Falls, NY. Sixty-eight women, including Elizabeth Cady Stanton and Lucretia Mott, and thirty-two men signed a Declaration of Sentiments, calling for the right of women to vote and to own property.

Thousand Islands

As a part of New York's northern coastline,
the St. Lawrence has islands divine.
But when Troy started counting
to give an accounting,
he could find only nine ninety-nine.

Historical Highlight: There are almost 1800 islands in the St. Lawrence River, which forms part of the boundary between New York State and Ontario, Canada. In order to be classified as part of the Thousand Islands, a land mass must be at least one square foot in area, be above water all year, and support one living tree.

Tuxedo Park

In Tuxedo Park, tobacco money
built a fine resort.

Pierre Lorillard the fourth erected the
finest club that had the
finest boathouse next to the
finest racetrack adjacent to the
finest golf course on the
finest land north of Manhattan.

Associating only with the finest Americans
(and the Duke of Windsor)
he designed the finest clothes
to be worn at the Autumn Ball.

Black satin stripes down the pants.
White cuffs at the wrists.
Cummerbund at the waist.
Black bowtie at the neck.

Who said he looked like a penguin?

Historical Highlight: In 1886, Pierre Lorillard IV designed the first tuxedo to be worn at his Autumn Ball. Some people think he took the design from a jacket worn by the Duke of Windsor.

tug hill tug
tug hill tug hill tug hil
hill tug hill tug hill
tug hill tug
hill tug hill
tug hill tug hill tug
hill tug hill tug
sledding

Tug Hill Snow Day

Hip, Hip, Hooray!
It's a snow day!
It's a
    hookey playing, home staying
    bed jumping, pillow plumping
    puzzle doing, TV viewing
    cookie baking, craft making
    cocoa drinking, ice rinking
    blanket hugging, unplugging
    pajama wearing, Teddy bearing
    igloo building, tummy filling
    snowball throwing, fire glowing
    downhill sledding, text sending
    story telling, Mother yelling
    icicle licking,
    tongue
    sthicking
kind of day.
Thip! Thip! Hooray!

Historical Highlight: The Tug Hill Plateau, which lies between the eastern end of Lake Ontario and the Adirondack Mountains, averages over three hundred inches of snow a year.

The Utica Union Suit

The old union suit makes for great underwear.
Just be sure that you button it up with care.
If your fireman's flap
should begin to unsnap,
you'll be walking around with your bottom bare.

Historical Highlight: The union suit was created in Utica, NY. The traditional version of this type of long underwear is red flannel with buttons down the front and a flap in the back.

Underground Railroad

The Underground Railroad was invisible
except to people who had seen enough
injustice and saw a way to fight it.

Conductors like Miz Tubman led passengers
by cover of night from
Elmira to
Ithaca,
Auburn,
Syracuse,
Oswego,
bound for Canada and freedom,
unbound from chains and ignorance.

Hopping station to station,
hiding under stair cupboards,
wading in water to deter bloodhounds,
eating just enough crumbs to stay alive,
they made it to the border of a
new place,
new name,
new job,
new life.

Historical Highlight: The Underground Railroad route from Elmira to Ithaca, Auburn, Syracuse, Oswego, and then on to Lake Ontario was only one of eight routes that 19th century slaves used to cross New York State on their way to freedom in Canada.

upstate downstate apples
upstate downstate apples
upstate downstate apples
upstate downstate apples
upstate downstate apples
upstate downstate apples

Upstate, Downstate

Upstate apples grow in orchards
of almost straight rows
on almost even ground.
Nestled under the protective arm
of the great lake,
they become ripe in due season.
Every bite nourishes our bodies,
builds our bones and
keeps our digestive systems crunching right along.

Downstate Apples sit on desks
in almost straight rows
in almost every school.
Under florescent lights and
the Board of Education
they become tools of transformation.
Every byte nourishes our minds,
expands our domain and
keeps our brain waves buzzing right along.

What say we meet in Albany for applesauce?

Historical Highlight: New York is the second largest apple producing state in the U.S. (first is Washington). The world's largest apple peel was created by Kathy Wafter Madison on October 16, 1976, in Rochester, NY. It was 172 feet 4 inches long.

Vassar College Observatory

Bold
girls
peering
through fractured
lenses time-travel
light-years ahead to discover
new stars; old careers lost in the flotsam and jetsam.

Historical Highlight: Vassar College Observatory is a National Historic Landmark in Poughkeepsie, NY. Finished in 1865, it was the first building on the Vassar College campus and the home and laboratory of Maria Mitchell, the first recognized female astronomer in the U.S.

Valentine Flats

Shh! I know a secret place.

Skip along Cattaraugus Creek,
take five giant steps down Grape Alley,
tag a few sycamore or walnut trees,
play Paper, Rock, Scissors with Gowanda Shale,
march through the marsh,
leapfrog past Bare Butt Falls.

Then lie on your back in the former farmland
and unplant your mind.
            Take leave from the Wii.
            Forget the TV.
Look up the limestone cliffs to watch
red hawks fly frames
around cloud pictures.
Drop some raspberries in your mouth and
let the juice drool down your chin.
Stay as long as you can in this secret place.

Adulthood comes too soon.

Historical Highlight: Shh! Don't tell anyone that Valentine Flats is part of the Zoar Valley in Western New York, south of Buffalo. The Cattaraugus Creek forms the boundary between Erie and Cattaraugus Counties.

víne
valley víne
valley víne valley
valley víne valley
víne valley

Vine Valley

How to Grow Grapes (or children)

Start with sturdy stock and healthy soil,
but be patient –
it takes a few years to get a vineyard growing.
When canes finally sprout,
tie them to the trunk so they grow straight.
Don't shadow them –
grapes need plenty of sun.
Be sure to fertilize, immunize, and supervise,
but don't brutalize, pulverize, or terrorize.
Pray that the good Lord rains down blessings,
and don't be afraid to prune
stalks that are running wild –
pruning makes plants stronger.
At graduation,
when the grapes have reached full size and look mature,
cut off your fruit,
but leave part of the stem attached to your vine.
Then, sit on your porch and savor the fruit of your labor.

Historical Highlight: New York State is third in the nation in grape production and has four major wine producing areas: Lake Erie, Finger Lakes, Hudson River Valley, and eastern Long Island.

Woodstock

Max Yasgur gave a party.
All us hippie kids were there.
We came creating traffic jams
with flowers in our hair.

We tented to the music,
folk and rock and psychedelic.
It rained and rained, and then it poured,
but all was copacetic.

From Havens down to Hendrix
we grooved all weekend long.
When peace and love are king and queen,
The Sixties still rock on.

Historical Highlight: The Woodstock Music and Arts Fair was held on a dairy farm in Bethel, NY, Aug. 15–18, 1969. Over 400,000 people camped in the mud to hear the folk and rock music stars of the day.

Waterloo Memorial

Can you spare one moment?
One moment of one day,
for those who gave up years of life
to keep us free today.

They wore hard soldiers' helmets.
They dressed in sailors' white.
They flew on U.S. Air Force wing
and ne'er gave up the fight.

At Normandy and Inchon Bay,
Afghanistan, Verdun.
In Baghdad and in Gettysburg
their sacrificing done.

Some dressed in privates' khaki,
Some sported generals' stars,
Some never held a weapon
but are heroes of those wars.

So won't you spare one moment?
To bow your head and pray,
or simply to remember those
who died for us today.

Historical Highlight: Waterloo, NY, has been nationally recognized as the birthplace of Memorial Day, which was first observed there on May 5, 1866 as a day to honor and remember those who had died in the Civil War.

methane gas methane gas
methane gas methane gas
methane gas
methane gas
thane gas methan
thane gas methan
thane gas methane

Wyoming County Dairy Farms

If you're talking energy,
raise Guernseys and you'll get it free.
We're talking Cow Power!
You can be sure,
if you're full of manure,
You've got Cow Power!
It may sound batty,
but burn that brown patty
To get Cow Power!
You get pure methane gas
out a calf's sassafras.
It's called Cow Power!
Nothing will reek
unless the pipe leaks.
Go with Cow Power!

As for windmills – too slow.
Solar panels? It snows.
Oil? Overdone.
Geothermal? No fun.

Don't be afraid.
Join the crusade.
It's all ready-made,
Cow Power!

Historical Highlight: Wyoming County has more cows than people and helps to make New York State the third largest producer of dairy products in the nation. Farmers are experimenting now to use cow manure to produce energy in the form of methane gas.

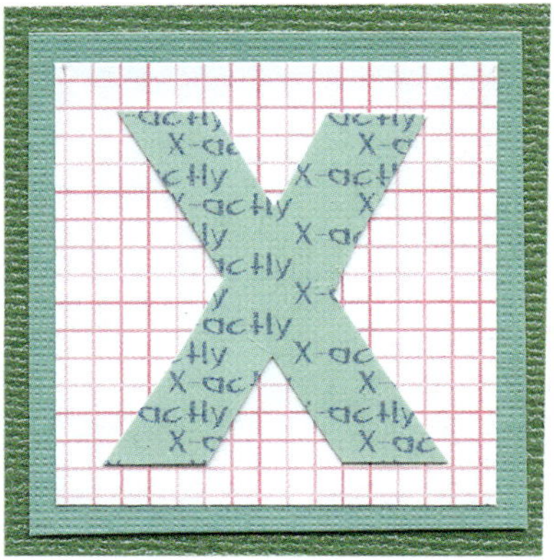

Xerox

Thanks to Xerography words copy easily.
Thanks to Xerography words copy easily.
Thanks to Xerography words copy easily.
Thanks to Xerography words copy easily.
Thanks to Xerography words copy easily.
Thanks to Xerography words copy easily.

Historical Highlight: Xerography (a combination of electrostatic printing and photography) was invented by Chester Carlson in Queens, NY, on October 22, 1938. The first business copier was made in 1959 in Rochester, NY, by the Haloid Co., which is now Xerox Corp.

X

Let X be the spot where you'll make your mark,
form a new formula, spike a new spark.
Unknown right now, you don't have a clue,
but someday New York will be so proud of you.

New York is a state of expert explorers.
We've no use for snivelers, snorters and snorers.
We exhibit exception, excel at extreme.
We build up, we gild up, no give up, we gleam.

With sixty-two counties, we've plenty of room
for you to take root and then start to bloom.
Let X mark your spot, not T, Y, or Z.
Your success is assured. It's a fait accompli.

Historical Highlight: New York State's motto is Excelsior, meaning ever upward.

coccinella novemnotata

X-actly

X-actly where is the ladybug?
the ladybug of New York fame,
the crop friendly nine-spotted ladybug,
Coccinella novemnotata by name.

X-actly where is the ladybug?
It's hard to believe we've lost her.
Where has New York's ladybug gone?
Haven't you come across her?

Is she under that rock?
No, it's just a red sock.
Is she on that oak tree?
Can't you see, it's a flea?
Is she there on the leaf?
It's beyond all belief.

X-actly where is the ladybug?
Make an X wherever you find her.

Then give her a kiss.
Make a quick wish.
And take off and follow behind her.

Historical Highlight: Coccinella novemnotata, the nine-spotted ladybug, was named New York State's official insect in 1989. Unfortunately, this particular ladybug has not been seen in a while. Cornell University is asking kids to send them a digital picture if they find the C-9 ladybug. For more information check out www.lostladybug.org.

Yeshiva University

If you want to succeed at Yeshiva,
wear your yarmulke just like the best.
Study Talmud and Torah intensely,
and put that great brain to the test.

Historical Highlight: Yeshiva University opened in 1928 in the Washington Heights area of New York City as a school where students could combine secular and religious studies.

Yonkers

I'm just bonkers over Yonkers
since Van der Doncker came around.
I'm just twitty for this city
where Otis had his ups and downs.

I'm all zonkers for the jonker
who plonked his plot right here,
started up a brand new sawmill,
set a lot of things in gear.

Sit me on a Smith-loomed carpet.
serve me on a Bake-lite plate,
let me golf at new St. Andrews.
Where else can you find life this great?

I'm just bonkers over Yonkers;
it's a town to emulate.
I'm just zonkers over Yonkers;
living here is still first rate.

Historical Highlight: The name Yonkers comes from the Dutch word jonker, which means young gentleman. Adriaen Van der Donck was the jonker who built a sawmill here when New York was called New Netherlands and belonged to the Dutch.

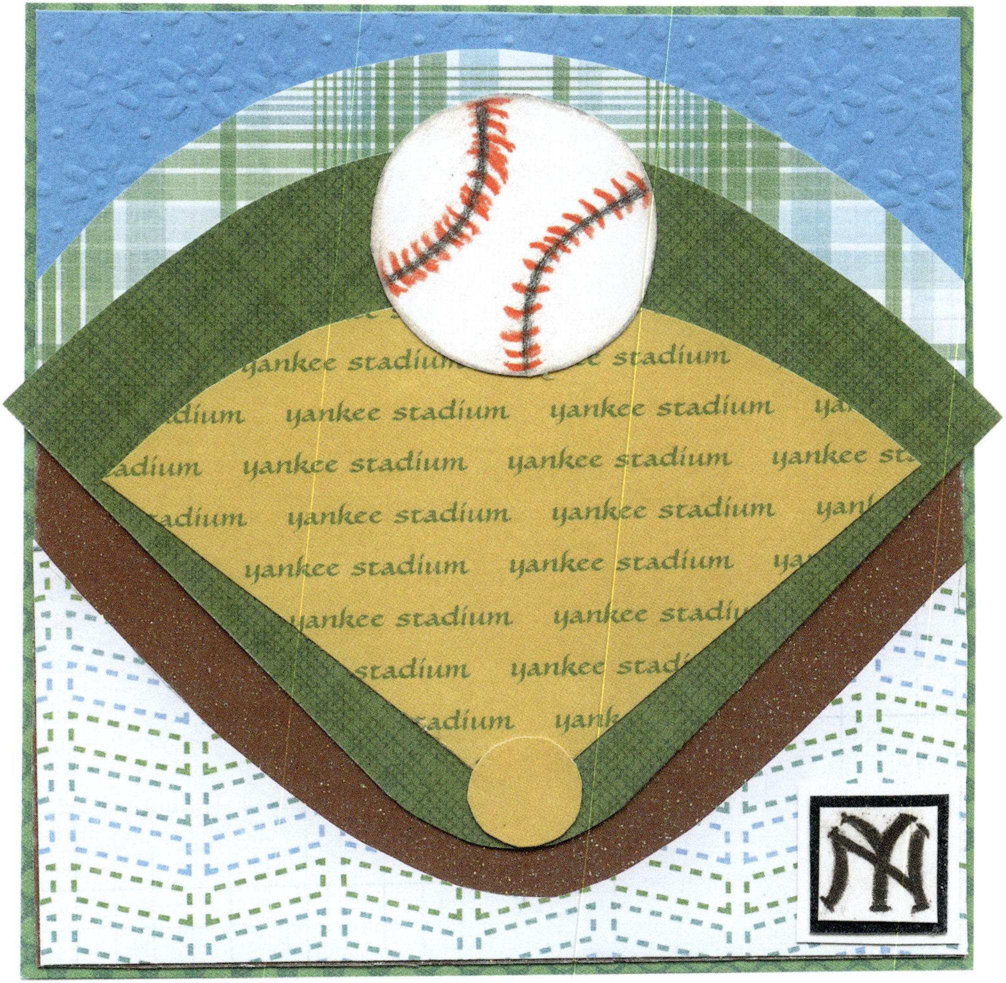
yankee stadium yankee stadium
yankee stadium yankee stadium
yankee stadium yankee stadium
yankee stadium yankee stadium
yankee stadium
stadium

Yankee Stadium

They say the ghosts of Baseball Past still
haunt the house that Ruth built,
that the six Yankees of Murderers' Row still
run the bases in order,
Combs to Lazzeri, while
Joltin' Joe continues his now
1,279,356 game winning streak.
Maris and Mantle still
vie for home run records as
Mr. October hits his fourth one of the game.
There's Larsen on the mound pitching a no-hitter
side by side with Guidry striking out Angels
while Yogi (glove open and mouth closed)
catches speedballs behind the plate.

If you listen real hard you can still hear the echo
of Gehrig's luckiest man speech
harmonizing with Merrill's national anthem and
Allen's radio commentary.

And they say that every now and then
on a warm summer night
when the moon and the house are both full,
The Babe himself shows up.
He lumbers to the plate,
picks up Reddish Bella in his left hand and
swings for the fences.
The Orioles, Cardinals, and Blue Jays
all dip their wings in salute.
The stars move out of the way and
the bleachers creak Amen.

Historical Highlight: Yankee Stadium was opened in 1923 in the Bronx with the first pitch thrown out by NY Governor Al Smith. It cost $2.4 million. Although renovated in the 1970s, the stadium was replaced with a new stadium in 2009 and torn down in 2010. The land under the old stadium will become a park called Heritage Field.

Zee End

If you're going from Zena to Zurich,
you'll find that it's not a short-haul.
Get your compass ready to zig-zag
cause there's no direct route there at all.

Historical Highlight: Zena and Zurich are the only places in New York State that begin with Z. Zena, in Ulster County, was named for a woman, and Zurich, in Wayne County, was named for the city in Switzerland. They are about 250 miles apart.

Ground Zero

The twin towers took years to build.
Founded on bedrock and gold bars,
ten thousand craftsmen engineered
a monument to trumpet
Empire State's success.

Thousands of tons of steel they welded.
Thousands of yards of concrete they poured
Thousands of joints they bolted securely
to create duel masterpieces,
tubes of lustrous silver
towering over Manhattan and the world.

The twin towers took years to build
and only minutes to fall down,
and only minutes to fall down.

Historical Highlight: The twin towers of the World Trade Center in New York City took seven years to build, from 1966 –1973. They withstood a fire on February 13, 1975 and a terrorist attack on February 26, 1993, but collapsed from a second terrorist attack on September 11, 2001.

Bronx Zoo
Bronx Zoo
BRONX ZOO

The Bronx Zoo

What if the animals lived alphabetical?
Anteaters, bears, chimpanzees.
Dodos and elephants, ferrets, gnus.
That's good news I'd sure like to see.

Ibex and ibis would follow the hyrax,
jerboa around the next bend.
Kangaroos, llamas there with their mamas,
macaws before mynahs, how zen!

Newts next to otters and pythons by quetzel,
rheas and rhinos, what fun!
Sheep, snakes and storks, and tortoises, too.
A unicorn if they can find one.

That leaves the voles, the vultures, the wallabies,
xerus, yaks, and zebus.
Wouldn't it be so copacetic, poetical,
Syncretic, aesthetic, and hyperkinetical,
if the Bronx had an all alphabetical zoo?

Historical Highlight: Dating back to 1899, the Bronx Zoo is the largest metropolitan zoo in the United States. Its 265 acres hold more than 4,000 animals.

Author's Note

New York is a wonderfully diverse state, with a rich history, beautiful geography, and colorful people and customs. These poems are intended to be a reflection and a celebration of the people and places in our great state. I have been to many, but not all, of the places mentioned in the poems, and they all have their own unique beauty. Readers, I encourage each of you to travel New York and experience life here for yourself.

If you'd like more information about place-names in New York, check out this reference:

Vasiliev, Ren. *From Abbotts to Zurich, New York State Placenames.* Syracuse, NY: Syracuse University Press, 2004.

This book has been a labor of love, and I have to thank all the usual suspects starting with my family: Gary, Kristen and David, Robyn and Tom. The book would not be the same without the creative illustrations done by my sister-in-law, Sue Valentine. They really make the poems come alive. Thanks also to the Night Writers critique group in Rochester who read the poems early on before there was a book or even a collection. Thanks also to Brianna Collier who provided me with a student's perspective. Again, as usual, thanks to my friend and proofreader, Faith Weidman, and editor/graphic designer Zach Steffen.

About the Author

Sally Valentine is a native Rochesterian who has been both a student and a teacher in the Rochester City School District. She is now off on a tangent of writing, and is the author of a series of novels for middle grade students, each set in a different Rochester landmark. The titles thus far are *The Ghost of the Charlotte Lighthouse*, *Theft at George Eastman House*, *What Stinks? An Adventure in Highland Park*, and *Lost at Seabreeze*.

You may contact Ms. Valentine on her website, www.RochesterAuthor.com, where you will also find her blog, "Stepping Around Rochester," and worksheets to go with each book. Teachers who wish to use the books to supplement their social studies curriculum may download the free worksheets and also contact her there for school visits. There are now poetry worksheets to go with this book.

Ms. Valentine is currently at work on more books in the Rochester series. Check out her website for publication dates.

About the Illustrator

Suzanne Valentine, more familiarly known to family and friends as Sue or Susie, has always had a keen interest in art. Her paternal grandmother was an oil painter, and was an inspiration to Sue when she was a young girl and teenager. Sue took art classes in high school, but then went off to college to study nursing at Georgetown University. Sue practiced many different kinds of nursing during her career, such as Critical Care, Community Health, Case Management, and Urgent Care. But, she always enjoyed some form of art as a hobby and stress reliever during her working years. She also spent many hours with her daughter (now grown!), making do-it-yourself art projects and crafts. Over the past few years she has enjoyed beading/jewelry making, colored pencil drawing, paper collage art and card making.

Her collaboration with her sister-in-law, Sally Valentine, has given Sue many hours of joy, especially those spent creating the colored pencil drawings for *What Stinks?* and *Lost at Seabreeze*. Their most current project, this book of children's poems entitled *There Are No Buffalo in Buffalo*, allowed Sue the chance to work in one of her favorite mediums, paper collage. To quote Sue, "The process of choosing the color, pattern, texture and various shapes for the poetry pictures has been a really fun and exciting process. Seeing the finished product is so rewarding, and I hope both the poetry and pictures will be enjoyed by children of all ages!"

Sue lives in Rochester, New York with her husband, a retired City of Rochester Firefighter.